TIDE POOL

WEBS OF LIFE

TIDE POOL

Paul Fleisher

BENCHMARK BOOKS

MARSHALL CAVENDISH
NEW YORK

The author would like to acknowledge Paul Sieswerda of the New York Aquarium for his careful reading. The author also acknowledges the support that his wife, Debra, has provided as he has researched and written this book. And finally, the author thanks his editor, Kate Nunn.

Benchmark Books
Marshall Cavendish Corporation
99 White Plains Road
Tarrytown, New York 10591-9001

Illustration by Jean Cassels

Library of Congress Cataloging-in-Publication Data
Fleisher, Paul.
Tide pool / Paul Fleisher.
   p.   cm. — (Webs of life)
Includes bibliographical references (p. 39) and index.
Summary: Describes how tide pools are formed and some of the plants and animals that can be found in them.
!SBN 0-7614-0431-7 (lib. bdg)
1. Tide pool ecology—Juvenile literature. 2. Tide pools—Juvenile literature. [l. Tide pools. 2. Tide pool ecology. 3. Ecology.] I. Title. II. Series.
QH541.5.S35F58   1988   574.5'2636—dc20   96-29171   CIP   AC

Photo research by Ellen Barrett Dudley

Cover photo: *Photo Researchers, Inc. / The National Audubon Society Collection / Renee Purse*

The photographs in this book are used by permission and through the courtesy of: *Photo Researchers, Inc./The National Audubon Society Collection*: Nancy Sefton, 2, 21, 27 (bottom); Jim Zipp, 6-7, 10-11, 24; Pat and Tom Leeson, 8-9; William H. Mullins, 15; Anne White, 18 (top); Farrell Grehan, 20; F. Stuart Westmorland, 25, 26, 28-29; Neil G. McDaniel, 30; Andrew Martinez, 32. *Brandon D. Cole*: 12, 13. *Animals Animals/Earth Scenes*: Anne Wertheim, 14, 23; E.R. Degginger, 16; Roger and Donna Aitkenhead, 17; Robert P. Comport, 34-35. *Peter Arnold*: Ed Reschke, 18 (bottom), 33; Fred Bavendam, 27 (top), 29. *Photo Researchers, Inc./Biophoto Associates/Science Source*: 19. *Tom Stack & Associates*: Mike Bacon, 22; Brian Parker, 31.

Printed in the United States of America

6   5   4   3   2   1

For Debra

The ocean waves have worn a hollow in the rocks of the Pacific coast. When the tide comes in, the rocks are covered with water. When the tide goes out, a small pool of seawater is left behind. A community of animals and plants live their whole lives in this pool. It is their world.

A tide pool is not an easy place for plants and animals to live. The waves pound against the rocks. In summer, the hot sun beats down, and in winter, chill winds blow.

Ocean waters rise and fall about twice a day. We call this motion the tide. The earth, moon, and sun pull on one another with the force of gravity. This pull causes the tides. Along the Pacific coast, there can be a difference of ten feet or more between low tide and high tide.

At high tide, the pool is covered with seawater. The waves crash against the shore and mix air into the water. There is plenty of oxygen for the sea creatures to breathe.

Six hours later, the tide is low and the pool is uncovered. For the creatures in the tide pool, the whole world changes. The sun warms the water in the hollowed-out rock. Warm water holds less oxygen than cold water. The plants and animals must survive the higher temperature and thinner air in the pool. Many creatures are no longer covered by water at all.

Which creatures live in a pool depends on how long the pool stays uncovered when the tide goes out. More kinds of plants and animals live in tide pools that are uncovered for only a short time. Pools higher up on the rocks have fewer kinds of life.

When the tide is out, we can walk down to the tide pool to look. Above the high tide line is the spray zone. The rocks are damp with spray from the breaking waves.

Be careful! The rocks are very slippery. They're covered with black and green algae. Algae are very simple plants. They don't have leaves or flowers. Like other plants, they make their own food. All they need is air, water, and the energy from sunlight.

12

Let's walk a little lower. Hundreds of periwinkles are crawling on the rocks. These snails spend most of their time out of the water. They scrape the algae off the rocks with their tongues. Periwinkles get wet for only a short time twice each day. They hold water inside their shells the rest of the time.

PERIWINKLES (TINY BLACK SNAILS) AND LIMPETS

BARNACLES

Acorn barnacles live just below the tide line. They don't move at all. They live inside a hard shell attached to the rock.

Barnacles are related to crabs and shrimp. When the tide covers them, barnacles open the little inner doors in their shells. They capture tiny swimming animals with their feet. When the tide falls, barnacles close their shells and wait.

14

The animals at the edge of this tide pool spend most of their time underwater.

Mussels live inside hard shells. When they are young, they attach themselves to the rock with tough threads.Once a mussel is attached, it never moves again.

Like barnacles, mussels open their shells when the tide rises. They take in seawater and filter out tiny plants and animals for food. When the tide goes out, the mussels close their shells.

BLUE MUSSELS

Some mussels have small crabs living inside their shells. Pea crabs don't hurt the mussel. They eat a little bit of the food that the mussel collects. Pea crabs don't have hard shells. They depend on the mussel's shell for protection.

PEA CRAB

PURPLE SHORE CRAB

Most crabs are hunters and scavengers. Scavengers eat dead plants and animals. Crabs have hard shells and strong pincers.

They spend much of the day hidden beneath the rocks. Now and then a purple shore crab scuttles out in search of food.

17

A dog whelk is a snail, like the periwinkle. But the whelk is a meat-eater. It bores a hole in the shell of a mussel or oyster with its tongue. Then it eats the animal inside.

DOG WHELK

FINGER LIMPET

A limpet is also a kind of snail. Like the periwinkle, it scrapes algae off the rocks. Each limpet has its own special home on the rocks. It returns to that spot when it has finished feeding on the algae. The limpet's shell fits tightly against the stone. Try to pry one away from the rock. It's almost impossible!

DIATOMS

Millions of tiny plants called diatoms live in the water. These one-celled algae are so small you need a microscope to see them. But there are so many diatoms that they make the ocean look green.

Diatoms use sunlight to make food. Like other algae, they make oxygen. Diatoms are very important to the web of life in the tide pool. Tiny animals eat them. Those tiny animals are food for the larger animals that we can see.

19

Seaweeds are another, larger kind of algae. They grow on the rocks, but they don't have roots. They get all the nutrients they need from the water around them. Seaweeds grip the rock with a flat holdfast. Like other plants, they need the sun's energy to make food. They can only grow where the water is shallow and there is plenty of light.

Sea lettuce is a bright green seaweed. It is so thin that sunlight shines right through it.

SEA LETTUCE

Rockweed is a tough, rubbery seaweed with little balloon-like air bladders. These float the rockweed up through the water toward the light.

There is lots of kelp in this tide pool. It has long, flat fronds that wave in the water. When the tide goes out, the seaweed drapes over the rocks.

Bright green surfgrass grows on the rocks, too.

ROCKWEED

LINED CHITON

Lift up a clump of rockweed. Look closely. You'll see snails, skeleton shrimp, and crabs crawling among the fronds. Animals hide in the rockweed to stay damp when the tide falls.

Like limpets, chitons (pronounced KY tunz) graze on the rocks. They are most active at night. During low tide they cling to the rocks under the seaweed or in a shady hollow.

23

GIANT GREEN ANEMONE

Look down now, through the water to the bottom of the pool. Sea anemones (uh NE muh neez) dot the rocky floor of the pool like bright flowers. But they are animals. A sea anemone attaches itself to the rock. To eat, the anemone captures small animals with its tentacles.

The tentacles have stinging cells, but the sting isn't strong enough to hurt a person. If you touch a sea anemone gently, it will protect itself by pulling in its tentacles. Anemones can move slowly, but most of the time they stay in one place.

A hermit crab makes its home in an empty snail shell. The shell protects its soft body from larger animals. The hermit crab is a scavenger. It crawls along, looking for dead plants and animals that have fallen to the bottom of the pool.

ORANGE HERMIT CRAB

Many of the rocks are coated with bright colors. These layers of orange, yellow, and red are animals. They are very simple creatures called sponges. Sponges filter small food particles from the water around them. Some sponges grow up from the rocks and form branching shapes. Others grow on the shells of snails or crabs.

YELLOW BORING SPONGE

BLUE-GREEN ALGAE AND ORANGE SPONGE

Sea stars cluster together on the floor of the tide pool. They have hundreds of little tubular feet. The feet are like tiny suction cups. Sea stars are hunters. They use their feet to pull mussel shells apart and eat the animals inside.

TUBE FEET OF SUNFLOWER STAR

29

SEA URCHIN

Sea urchins live at the bottom of the tide pool. The sea urchin scrapes algae, sponges, and other small animals from the rocks with its sharp beak. Bristly spines protect it from other animals. The sea urchin is a relative of the sea star. Turn it over and you will see that it, too, has many little tube feet.

The animal in this tube is a feather duster worm. It uses its feathery tentacles to filter small animals out of the water to eat. As the worm grows bigger, it builds a bigger tube. The worm pulls back into its tube when a larger animal passes by or when the water gets too low or too rough.

GIANT FEATHER DUSTER

Small fish called tide pool sculpins live in this pool. A tide pool is not a safe place for a fish. Gulls, terns, and other birds patrol the pool, on the lookout for a meal. When the tide is out, the sculpin hides quietly in the liquid shadows. Its camouflage makes it hard to see.

EFT: SCULPIN   WESTERN GULL

Soon the tide begins to rise again. Unless we want to get wet, it's time for us to leave. Waves break across the tide pool. The cold ocean water is full of oxygen and full of food.

In a few minutes the pool becomes part of the ocean. Beneath the waves, life in the tide pool goes on.

Later, when the tide goes out again, the tide pool and the creatures living in it will be uncovered once more for us to see.

Can you name the plants and animals in this tide pool?

Turn the page to check your answers.

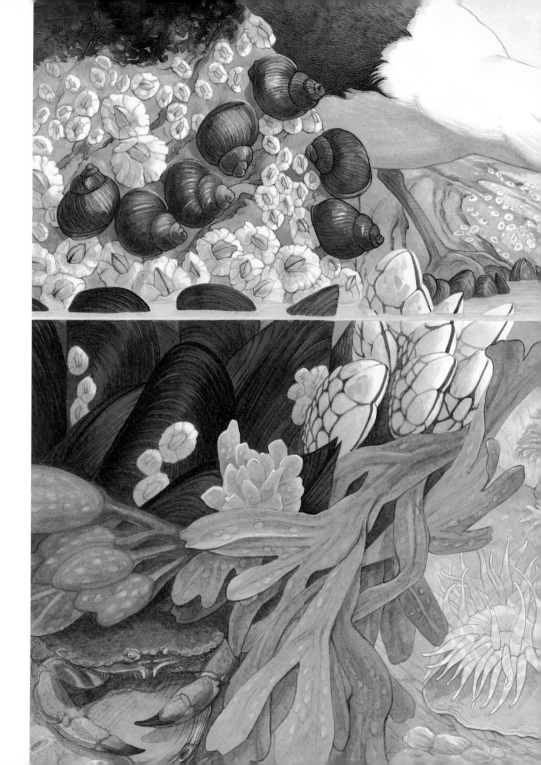

Plants and Animals Found in This Tide Pool

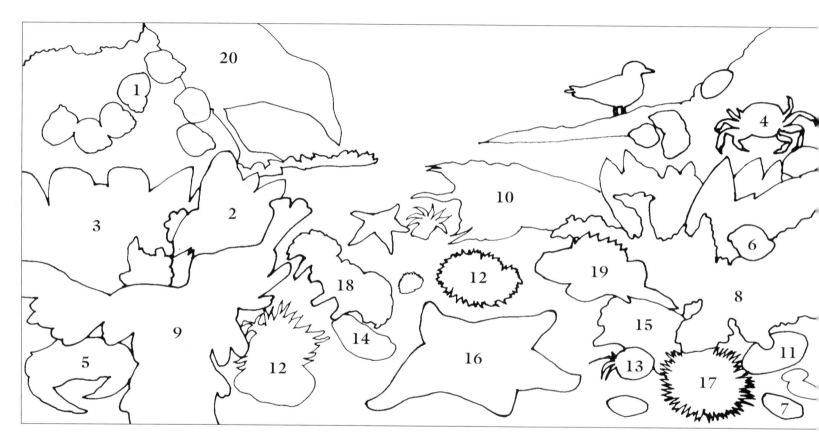

1. periwinkle
2. acorn barnacle
3. mussel
4. shore crab
5. rock crab

6. dog whelk
7. limpet
8. sea lettuce
9. rockweed
10. kelp

11. chiton
12. sea anemone
13. hermit crab
14. yellow sponge
15. red sponge

16. sea star
17. sea urchin
18. feather duster worm
19. sculpin
20. sea gull

FIND OUT MORE

Bowden, Joan. *Why the Tides Ebb and Flow.* New York: Houghton Mifflin, 1990.

Gunzi, Christiane. *Tide Pool.* New York: Dorling Kindersley, 1992.

Malnig, Anita. *Where the Waves Break: Life at the Edge of the Sea.* Minneapolis: Carolrhoda, 1985.

Rood, Ronald, and Martin Classen. illus. *Tide Pools.* New York: HarperCollins Children's Books, 1993.

INDEX

ABOUT THE AUTHOR

In addition to writing children's books, Paul Fleisher teaches gifted middle school students in Richmond, Virginia. He spends many hours outdoors, gardening or fishing on the Chesapeake Bay. His trips to explore the environment include a recent visit to the tide pools of the Pacific Coast.

Fleisher is active in organizations that work for peace and social justice, including the Richmond Peace Education Center and the Virginia Forum.